"This is an excellent book and re[...] journey. The book is very interac[...] students to process their faith thro[...] ties. Author Amy Simpson takes a very difficult concept and through discovery learning allows the reader an opportunity to encounter God. It is an incredible resource for individuals as well as one that could be used in youth ministry as small-group curriculum or in mentoring relationships."

—MARTI BURGER, director of youth and family ministries,
Evangelical Covenant Church

> INTO THE WORD

HOW TO GET THE MOST FROM YOUR BIBLE

AMY SIMPSON

NAVPRESS ®

For a free catalog
of NavPress books & Bible studies call
1-800-366-7788 (USA) or 1-800-839-4769 (Canada).

www.NavPress.com

Into the Word content previously published in *In the Word: Bible Study Basics for Youth Ministry*, Copyright 2004 by Amy Simpson.

ISBN-10: 1-60006-094-3
ISBN-13: 978-1-60006-094-6

Cover design by studiogearbox.com
Cover image by VEER, Kristopher Grunert
Creative Team: Rebekah Guzman, Candace McMahan, Cara Iverson, Darla Hightower, Arvid Wallen, Pat Reinheimer

Some of the anecdotal illustrations in this book are true to life and are included with the permission of the persons involved. All other illustrations are composites of real situations, and any resemblance to people living or dead is coincidental.

All Scripture quotations in this publication are taken from the HOLY BIBLE: NEW INTERNATIONAL VERSION® (NIV®). Copyright © 1973, 1978, 1984 by International Bible Society. Used by permission of Zondervan Publishing House. All rights reserved.

Printed in the United States of America

1 2 3 4 5 6 7 8 9 10 / 12 11 10 09 08

> >   >

CONTENTS

Introduction 7

Chapter 1: The Ultimate Travel Guide 9

Chapter 2: Learning to Navigate. 21

Chapter 3: Equipped for Adventure 35

Chapter 4: Hitting the Trail 41

Chapter 5: Extreme Adventure 49

Discussion Guide. 77

Author 79

INTRODUCTION

Do you realize that we have more access to more information (more quickly) than anyone else in human history? There's a reason they call this the Information Age! At the click of a mouse, we can find information about almost anything, read about the thoughts and ideas of someone halfway across the world, buy nearly anything, spend time with friends, and let the world get to know us. We can communicate instantly, all while sitting in the same place. In fact, we are literally bombarded with information. Our brains are constantly making decisions to ignore most of the information we encounter.

This sort of information-rich society didn't exist a couple of decades ago. Previous generations could only dream of what we experience every day. No one has ever *known* so much.

And yet your generation is perhaps the most biblically illiterate since the printing press.

Why? Is it because today's teenagers are incapable of learning about the Bible? Of course not! Because you don't have access to Bibles to read for yourselves? No way! You don't have access to tools to help you study the Bible? On the contrary! The problem is that teenagers, like everyone else, need to be taught how to study, understand, and apply the Bible. And that kind of understanding doesn't happen instantly.

In this world of instant and constant communication, we're fascinated with the value of our own words. But what about God's Word? The Bible's messages are timeless, spoken to every generation. They are boundless, touching the hearts of people in every part of the world. And they are powerful, changing lives every day.

If you want to experience the power of God's Word in your life, you'll need to learn to know, love, and live the Bible.

This book will help you do just that. *Into the Word* is a basic introduction to the Bible and how to study it for yourself. This book includes five chapters:

Chapter 1: The Ultimate Travel Guide will teach you where the Bible came from and why you should study it.

Chapter 2: Learning to Navigate will teach you a simple Bible study method that will help you understand what you read.

Chapter 3: Equipped for Adventure will give you a basic understanding of some study tools you can use to better understand God's Word.

Chapter 4: Hitting the Trail will help you focus on application, making sure you do more than read God's Word; you apply it to your life and act on it.

Chapter 5: Extreme Adventure gives you a chance to put into motion what you learn in the first four chapters, with specific Bible study projects and a journal for your insights as you study the Bible.

Go ahead and get into God's Word. There's no better way to experience God's power to change the way you live. I hope this book will inspire you to make Bible study a lifelong adventure. As you read it and use the ideas, you'll welcome God's truth into your life. See what happens!

CHAPTER 1

THE ULTIMATE TRAVEL GUIDE

So what's the big deal about the Bible? Is it just another book? A collection of people's thoughts and stories? Did God actually write it? Where did it come from, and why should you care what it says?

The Bible is a very special and critically important book, and not because it's sometimes printed on gold-trimmed pages and bound in leather. The Bible's importance and authority come from God. Studying the Bible can literally help you know God. It can change your life. Most people want God's power and presence in their lives, but many are suspicious of the Bible — can they really trust what it says? So before you study the Bible, it's important to understand how it came about, who wrote it, and the circumstances under which it was written. I'm confident that the deeper you delve into God's Word, the more you'll find it to be valid and trustworthy.

In this chapter, you'll learn that the Bible is rooted in context. That means it didn't just spring up from nowhere. And understanding where it came from can help you understand what it means. You'll learn where the Bible came from and why you should study it. And you might gain a new respect for this living, active message from God.

STARTING THE JOURNEY

Take a few minutes to walk around your house. As you walk around, notice a few random objects. For each object, consider what gives that object credibility and value and makes it trustworthy. For example, maybe you'll see a history book in your room. You might decide that book has credibility because it describes events as they happened according to people who witnessed them. You probably have a loaf of bread in your kitchen. You might decide a loaf of bread has value because it satisfies hunger. Make sure one of the objects you consider is a Bible.

As you walk around and evaluate objects, use the space below to write notes about your observations.

You may not do this actual activity on a regular basis, but what you may not realize is that you do this kind of evaluation all the time. Every day you have to decide whom and what to trust. For example, every time you sit down, you have to decide whether to trust the chair (and the person who made it!). Every time you set your alarm clock, you decide to trust that it will wake you at the right time.

So how do we determine whether something is credible and whether it has value in our lives? Most of us base our trust on what we know about the object, the person who made it, and the way we have experienced it in the past.

IN-DEPTH EXPLORATION

This section of the book will help you do this kind of evaluation with the Bible. In the next few pages, we're going to explore what gives the Bible credibility and value in our lives. The funny thing is, we're often more willing to trust some of these other objects than we are to trust the Bible itself. But the Bible has more credibility and value than any of these other things. Let's start by finding out more about what the Bible is and where it came from.

> WHERE THE BIBLE CAME FROM

So where did the Bible come from? Believe it or not, it truly did come from God. To create the Bible, God (through the Holy Spirit) directed people to pass along his messages to others. Some of them wrote down their messages right away, and others spoke their messages. Because the Holy Spirit inspired the writing of the Bible, the messages it contains are God's messages to people. The Bible reflects the perspectives of the various authors, but the truth is from God.

The Bible was written by more than forty people over the course of sixteen hundred years and sixty generations. These authors included a wide variety of people, such as fishermen, shepherds, kings, prophets, and pastors. They wrote their messages on three different continents — Asia, Africa, and Europe — and in many different places, such as prisons, palaces, the wilderness, and even a remote island. They wrote in three different languages: Hebrew, Aramaic, and Greek. The Bible we read was translated from these languages.

Even though the Bible was written over such a long period of time by so many different authors from such a diversity of backgrounds, God's Word is remarkably consistent in its themes. Throughout Scripture, we find one constant message: God loves us and wants us to have a relationship with him.

So I realize that it's sort of hard to understand what the Holy Spirit's inspiration might have been like. But the Bible's consistency, accuracy, and wisdom provide great evidence of this inspiration. The "Try This!" box describes a fun way you can think more about this.

TRY THIS!

If you have a friend around, try this idea to help you think more about where the Bible came from.

Grab a piece of paper, a pen, and a buddy. Sit back-to-back.

One of you tells the other person something to draw; then the other person draws that thing. Be sure you and your friend don't look at each other or at the drawing. Allow a few minutes for drawing.

Now switch. The other person tells what to draw while the partner draws it. Again, make sure you don't look at each other or the drawing.

After you finish drawing, look at each picture. Discuss these questions:

> **How close was the picture to the partner's instructions?**
> **How did the artist's personality and interpretation come through in the drawing?**
> **How might this compare to the way the Holy Spirit inspired people to write the Bible?**

> HOW THE BIBLE CAME TO BE

As the Holy Spirit inspired people to pass along God's messages to others, some of those people wrote down those messages right away. Others proclaimed God's messages through the spoken word, and those messages were passed down orally for generations. In those days, most people didn't learn to read and write in school the way we do. Instead, they learned by listening to stories told by their elders. They learned to recite these stories precisely. Since they didn't read and write, storytelling was the only way for them to record the events that happened to them and their people. This resulted in oral cultures rather than written cultures.

Eventually, strong written cultures developed. People began to write their stories and collect them. They began to value these stories in written form. The oral messages of the Bible were written down as well, and people began to gather all the writings together in hopes of distributing them for others to read. They had no way to print books at that time, so they copied the Scriptures by hand, being extremely careful not to make mistakes.

After a while, many different writings had been collected. Religious scholars began the process of canonization (deciding what should and should not be considered authoritative and Holy Scripture). Throughout centuries, people worked together to carefully evaluate various writings. They used lists of criteria to determine which books contained consistent messages and the authority to be considered God's Word. Basically, they used two main criteria: Had the book enjoyed widespread and long-standing approval among Christians? And had the book been written or approved by eyewitnesses to the events described? If the book was from the New Testament, it had to meet a third criterion: Had it been written or approved by Jesus' apostles (his original and personal followers)?

Scholars and church leaders spent centuries not only evaluating these writings but also meeting to discuss whether specific writings should be included. This process of canonization determined the collection of writings we know as the Bible. It is a collection written by firsthand witnesses and other reliable people who created their accounts through the inspiration of the Holy Spirit. All of these writings have stood the test of time, biblical scholarship, and faithful prayer for God's guidance.

So putting the Bible together was basically a long process of collecting and sorting, kind of like sorting a scattered stack of playing cards. Let's say you walk into a room and find a mess of playing cards on the floor. To clean up the mess and sort the cards, you would first need to collect them all. Then you would need to decide how to sort them. You would need some criteria. For example, you could put all of the numbered cards in one pile and the face cards in another. Or you could divide them into a black pile and a red pile. Or you could find all the cards with numbers that are included in your birth date.

Okay, so maybe this sorting process isn't quite like the process of canonizing the Bible, but it gives the basic idea about using specific criteria to make a decision. The people who collected the Bible determined which books truly were inspired by the Holy Spirit, and in this process itself, they sought and received the Holy Spirit's guidance.

> PARTS OF THE BIBLE

The Bible is divided into two main sections: the Old Testament and the New Testament. The Old Testament was written before Jesus was born as a man on earth. The New Testament was written after Jesus' birth.

Within these two main sections, the Bible isn't just a storybook or a reference book; it's a collection of writings by various people at different times, in different places, and for different purposes. These individual writings include various types of literature, such as historical accounts, poetry, prophecies, letters, and proverbs (wise sayings).

Each individual book of the Bible is a different piece of writing that originally stood on its own. For example, the book of Romans was a letter written by the apostle Paul to some people who lived in Rome (Romans, get it?).

Within each book are further divisions called chapters, just as in any novel or textbook you might read. These chapter numbers and divisions were added by people who wanted to make the Bible easier for people to read and understand. They also added verses to make things easier to find. Reading individual chapters and verses can help us find specific things in the Bible and also understand where major themes and concepts are located. However, it's important to keep in mind that these were not part of the original writings, so they must be read in the context of each book as a whole. If you want to understand what a specific verse is about, it's important to understand what the entire book is about.

So to find something in the Bible, look for the book of the Bible (you can always use the table of contents in your Bible) and then locate the chapter and the specific verse. For example, if someone says to turn to Romans 12:4, you would turn to the book of Romans, chapter 12, verse 4. Note if the book is from the Old Testament or the New Testament, as this helps you put what you're reading into context with the time period in which it took place.

Finding something in the Bible is sort of like finding a place on a map. If you want to find something in your community, what's the first thing you need to know? The address, of course. Once you know a place's address, you can look on the map to figure out where it is (or use the Internet to get directions).

Scripture references are sort of like addresses. Knowing the reference helps you navigate the Bible to find the verse or passage. Practice now by looking up and reading these Scriptures:

- Acts 8:4
- Esther 4:16
- Exodus 20:8
- Haggai 2:6-7
- Hebrews 11:1
- Jude 20

Hey, you've just learned a lot about the Bible and why we might want to pay attention to what it says. You've also learned how to find what you need in the Bible. Let's learn more by looking at some of what the Bible says about itself.

BIBLE DISCOVERY

Use your navigational skills to find 2 Timothy 3:16-17. (Remember to start with the table of contents to find out whether 2 Timothy is in the Old or New Testament.) Then read what the Scripture passage has to say. Try reading it again; then write your answers to these questions:

> What does this Bible passage mean when it says, "All Scripture is God-breathed"?

> Why do you think God chose to inspire people to write the Bible instead of creating it in some other way?

> What does that say about the Bible's purpose and power?

According to 2 Timothy 3:16-17, the Bible is useful in four ways: teaching (helping us to learn God's truth), rebuking (showing us when we're wrong), correcting (showing us what is right), and training in righteousness (helping us choose what's right). Makes sense, huh? But how does the Bible do these things? Spend a few minutes thinking about that question, and then write your ideas below. Use the sample answers to get started. If you have a friend nearby, you might want to brainstorm together.

> Teaching
The Bible teaches us by telling us what Jesus' life was all about.

> Rebuking
The Bible rebukes by showing us when the way we are living is against what God wants for our lives.

> Correcting
The Bible corrects us by reminding us how God wants us to live.

> Training in Righteousness
The Bible tells us that God gives us wisdom when we ask him to.

Hopefully you were able to name some of the ways the Bible is useful in people's lives, just as the Bible says it is. If you're short on ideas, try asking several other people about how the Bible has helped them in these ways. Write down their answers too. You might be amazed to see how powerful God's Word is in the lives of people you know. The truth of the Bible really does have the power to change people's lives! Want to see God's truth change your life? Keep reading to consider how you can welcome the power of God's Word in your own life.

THE ADVENTURE CONTINUES

Grab a pen and get comfy. Get ready to spend some time quietly thinking and journaling about what you've learned so far. Consider the following questions and write your answers in the space provided:

> How should you respond to what you learned today about the Bible?

> Why should you trust the Bible? Value it? Study it?

> How do you feel about the Bible today? About God?

You've made some exciting discoveries! A great way to respond to these discoveries would be to learn more about God's Word and how you can study it. As you continue to work your way through this book, you'll explore how you can do your best to understand God's message through the Bible. Enjoy this great adventure!

CHAPTER 2

LEARNING TO NAVIGATE

Most people seem to think they know what the Bible is about, even if they've never really read it. And they're reluctant to read it, even if they're curious to know what it says.

Why? Well, people have lots of reasons for not reading the Bible. But many people don't read the Bible because they don't understand what it says. Or they may try to read the Bible but experience no joy or change as a result because they don't know what to do with it.

If this has been a problem for you, it doesn't have to be. In this chapter, you'll learn how to study and make sense of the Bible. You'll learn a Bible study process you can use to dive into God's Word and make the most of it.

STARTING THE JOURNEY

Before the Bible study, a small detour. Find a pencil and an eraser. Look at the coded message on the next page. See if you can figure out what it says. First try to crack the code; then decipher the message. If you need help, look at the "Clues" that follow the code. If you need more help after that, try "More Clues."

CODED MESSAGE

[coded symbols]

[coded symbols] 4:12

CLUES

◉ = a
❀ = t
◐ = o

MORE CLUES

◎ = s
✳ = i
✹ = d

Okay, time's up. Did you crack the code? Did you solve the message? Turn to page 24 to see the right answer.

Now stop to think for a second about how you felt as you tried to break this code. Have you ever had this same feeling when you were reading the Bible? Maybe you've felt frustrated because you didn't understand what you were reading. Maybe you've felt as if someone had actually written a coded message and it didn't make any sense to you. Many people feel this way when they read the Bible.

As you were working to crack the code, you probably used some clever strategies to figure out what the coded message meant. You may have started by figuring out what just one symbol meant. Then that helped you figure out another symbol. And another. As you worked to decipher the message, you gained more and more knowledge, and that knowledge helped you as you kept working.

Well, you can learn some strategies to help you understand the Bible as well. Reading the Bible doesn't have to feel like deciphering a coded message. It's time to learn about a method you can use to understand the Bible better. But before you move on, stop and pray that God will reveal his truth to you during your study and that he'll help you understand and get excited to study the Bible.

IN-DEPTH EXPLORATION

There are many ways to go about studying the Bible. This book will teach you a simple method that may help as you try to understand the Bible and experience its power in your life. It's called the S.T.O.P. method. Here it is:

THE S.T.O.P. METHOD FOR BIBLE STUDY

1. What does it SAY?
2. What were the TIMES?
3. What did it mean ORIGINALLY?
4. What does it mean for me PERSONALLY?

Let me describe each step of the process.

The first step involves the words in the Bible passage. Think about what the words actually say and look up the meanings of any words you don't know. Use a reliable source for this, such as a dictionary.

The second step is to consider what the times were like when the passage was written. What was the time period in history? What events were happening? What was important to people at that time? Again, it's a great idea to look up this information in a reliable source, such as a Bible encyclopedia. You'll find more information about this kind of Bible study tool in chapter 3.

The third step is to consider what the Bible passage meant when it was written. Think about who wrote it, who it was written for, and what it would have meant to the first people who received the message. A good study Bible can help you discover these things.

The last step is to think about how the Bible passage applies to you. Knowing what you learned in the other three steps, what can you learn and act on in your own life? What difference does it make to you?

It's a simple approach, but each step is important. This process will help you learn more about the meaning of any Bible passage you read. The best way for you to understand how this process works is to actually use it. Why not now? Take some time now to practice using this method, but not with the Bible yet. First you'll need to find a reliable dictionary, either in print or online.

Once you have your dictionary handy, read this:

As you amble across this vast orb, be mindful of the many favorable circumstances in which you might luxuriate in the diminutive sources of bliss in this commonplace existence.

Huh?

MESSAGE SOLUTION Here's the solution to the coded message:

For the word of God is living and active. Sharper than any double-edged sword, it penetrates even to dividing soul and spirit, joints and marrow; it judges the thoughts and attitudes of the heart.

Hebrews 4:12

Okay, don't panic. Here's your challenge: Use the first step of the S.T.O.P. method to evaluate this paragraph. Think about what each word means, and use the dictionary to look up any words you don't understand. Then rewrite the paragraph here in your own words:

Got it? Hopefully your "translation" says something like this:

As you walk through life on earth, be aware of opportunities to enjoy the little things in everyday life.

Cool, huh? When you first looked at the paragraph, it probably seemed like nonsense. But with some serious thought and effort (and a good dictionary), I bet you were able to figure out at least some of what it meant.

TRY THIS!

If you have some friends or family members nearby, challenge them to try this too. You can use these paragraphs:

Without exception, diurnally, it will behoove you to employ a policy of remaining qualified for any one happenstance with which you might conceivably rendezvous within the duration of that term.

[Translation: Every day, it's a good idea to be prepared for anything you might experience that day.]

At any suitable circumstance, ceaselessly pay heed to those venerable and seasoned sagacious veterans of earlier vintage who will of their own accord dispense their expansive prudence for your profit.

[Translation: Whenever you have a chance, always pay attention to older and more-experienced people who will give you helpful advice.]

Are you gaining confidence? Now try using the second step of the S.T.O.P method. Imagine that the following paragraphs were written sometime in the past. As you read them, look for clues to figure out what the times were like when this took place:

Samuel waited nervously in the parlor, glancing around the room as if to find some comfort in his surroundings. He was sure the fire in the fireplace was supposed to be warm and inviting, but it seemed cruel to him as he sat there, sweating in his stiff collar.

What had she said when the housemaid had told her he was in the parlor? He had received encouragement from her, he thought. She had seemed interested in him, and courting her in this way had seemed like the natural next step. But what if he had misread her? What if she didn't want his attentions?

He heard footsteps in the hallway, and he stood up and composed himself.

Hmmm . . . probably didn't happen at your house last week, unless you live in a very strange house. When do you think this would have taken place? Write your ideas here:

So when did this happen? Well, for starters, this happened a hundred years ago or more, when people had parlors and maids and "courting" was very formal. If you were going to try to understand what was written, it would be important to know what life was like back then.

TRY THIS!

Again, if you have friends or family around, have them try this step. Here are some writings you can use:

When the sun came up, Elizabeth grabbed the water bucket and set out for the well in the center of town. It was best, she had decided, to complete this chore before the sun grew too hot. It seemed like a much easier task in the early morning, when the cobblestones were still cool and the grass was wet with dew. She extinguished her lamp and stepped outside.

[This happened before electric lights and indoor plumbing were invented, and people had to work very hard for basic necessities of life.]

Rachel heaved the pot of potatoes into the back of the wagon with the tools and all four children. As she watched her husband finish hitching the team, she ran through her mental checklist. Had she forgotten anything?

It would be a long, exciting day — different from most Saturdays. They had been preparing all week, doing extra chores so they would be able to leave for the day.

They would head to the Jensen homestead and spend the day helping the family rebuild their barn. Poor Jensens, they had had a rough year — with the illness and the new baby, and now their barn burning down. But the neighbors would come together today, and by the end of the day they would have a new barn minus the finishing touches.

The horses were ready, Rachel's mental review was complete, and the family was ready to go. She climbed aboard the wagon and smiled at her children. It would be a rewarding day.

[This happened in frontier days, when people settled new lands and worked hard to build new communities.]

You're getting good at this. I can tell.

Now let's try the third step of the S.T.O.P. method. In this step, you'll think about what the writing meant when it was actually written. You'll have to consider who wrote it, who the person wrote it for, and what it meant to the reader.

> Dear Michael,
>
> I love you so much. Every day I think about you and long for the time when we will be together again. I miss you so much and can't wait to see you. I've never loved anyone as much as I love you.
>
> Yesterday I was at the mall and thought I saw you walking toward me. My heart skipped a beat . . . but it wasn't you. I was so disappointed.
>
> Please remember that I love you, and take good care of yourself. I'll be there soon!
>
> All my love,
> Emily

Who wrote this one, and who was it written to?

Well, this one is almost embarrassing. Hopefully you could tell that this was originally a very personal letter from a girlfriend or wife to a man she hadn't seen for a while. She was planning to see him again soon. And when Michael read this letter, he would have known that Emily loved him and missed him. And—unless he didn't feel the same way about her—he would have looked forward to seeing her.

Important to know, huh? If you didn't know all of this, you might read the words "I was so disappointed" differently. For example, you might think they were written by someone who was angry, cruel, or frustrated. But since you know Emily wrote the letter to Michael, someone she loved, you know that the words were written out of both sadness and love. In a similar way, people sometimes read individual sentences or paragraphs in the Bible and misunderstand what they mean because they don't understand who wrote them and who they were written to.

TRY THIS!

Grab someone else and try the third step. Use these letters:

Dear Mom and Dad,

Hi! I hope everything is going well at home. Things are going fine here. I'm doing fine in all my classes.

I met this girl. I want to take her out, but I don't have enough money to take her someplace nice. Also, my roommate's TV broke — sure wish I had one. Oh, remember those snacks you sent with me, Mom? I've really enjoyed them. They're almost gone, though.

I miss you guys. I would come home for a visit, but I'm a little short on gas money. I'll see you at Christmas!

Love,

Alex

[This was a letter from a college student to his parents. He hinted very strongly — and frequently — that he would like his parents to send him money.]

Dear Madison:

I like you. You are nice. You are cute, too. I hope you like me. Do you like me? Do you want to be my girlfriend? Please circle yes or no and send it back.

Yes   No

Love,
Andrew

Okay, one more step to go. Let's practice the fourth step of the S.T.O.P. method, thinking about what the Bible passage means for you personally. This one is not as much about the meaning of the individual words as it is about what you'll do as a result of reading them. After you read what it says, you'll have to decide why it matters to you. Try this one:

> Take 2 teaspoons every 6 to 8 hours as needed. Do not take more than 3 doses in 24 hours, or the following side effects may occur: headache, dizziness, nausea, mental confusion, tripping and falling, drowsiness, uncontrollable gas, seeing spots, hair loss, body odor, bad breath, tongue paralysis, and voracious appetite. Be cautious when operating heavy machinery.

Write your ideas here:

Well, perhaps many lessons can be gleaned from this piece of writing. Probably the most significant is this: These instructions indicate that a person would want to be very careful in taking this medication, or perhaps not take it at all, given the possible side effects. If I were reading this, I would probably decide that I'd better have a really good reason for taking this medication. Otherwise, I wouldn't take it.

TRY THIS!

Here are some instructions you can use to challenge someone else to use the fourth step of the S.T.O.P. method:

If you're coming from the east or the west, take the freeway through the city. Exit the freeway at 76th Street. Go north on 76th Street a couple of miles. Go east on Maple Street. Turn north on 10th Street. Go east on Market Street. Then go north on Park Avenue. Drive two blocks; then turn into the parking lot on the corner and park.

If you're coming from the north or the south, take 122nd Street into the city. Go east on Pacific Street. Turn north on 76th Street and go a couple of miles. Go east on Maple Street. Turn north on 10th Street. Go east on Market Street. Then go north on Park Avenue. Drive two blocks; then turn into the parking lot on the corner and park.

Be sure to be there on time or early. Doors close promptly at 9:00. You'll need the right password to get in, so call the night before to find out what the current password is.

See you there!

[These instructions make it pretty clear that a person would want to be prepared with the correct password and an idea of which direction he or she will be coming from. The person would definitely want to be on time, too.]

Before beginning assembly, make certain you have all the parts listed in the parts list.

Insert piece A into piece B and piece C into piece D. Connect pieces A and C by tying the nylon cord (piece E) through the hole in the end of each piece.

Assemble the base by connecting pieces F through L, in order. Attach to piece M as shown. Following the diagram, use pieces N through S to build the top of the unit. Connect the top, the bottom, and the base with piece T as shown.

To avoid risk of electric shock, keep away from water, power sources, static electricity, intense heat, corrosive substances, loud noises, alien life, and annoying people.

[According to these directions, a person will want to make sure all the parts are present and he or she understands the directions before starting the assembly process. A person would also want to be very careful in using the finished product. In fact, if the person lives with any annoying people or aliens, he or she probably wouldn't want to use it at all.]

How did you feel as you went through these steps? Hopefully you had a little fun and developed some confidence at the same time. Not so difficult, are they? If you can use these steps to understand the wacky writings in this book, you can use them to study and understand the Bible.

So take a deep breath before we get started. It's time to try using these steps to study a Bible passage.

BIBLE DISCOVERY

Find Luke 18:9-14 in your Bible. This is where you'll find Jesus' parable (story) about a Pharisee and a tax collector.

We'll leave out the fourth step for now. Pick one of the first three steps in the S.T.O.P. method that you'd like to practice now:

1. What does it SAY?
2. What were the TIMES?
3. What did it mean ORIGINALLY?

Once you've chosen the step you want to practice, get ready to spend a little time on it. Read Luke 18:9-14. Then practice using the step you've chosen. As you work, write your notes below.

Take a moment to sit back and read what you've learned. Not bad, huh? Feels pretty good to understand more about what you're reading. If you use them, all of these steps will help you understand more about what you read in the Bible. You can use this method every time you study the Bible.

Now it's time to go through all four steps. We'll use another Bible passage for this.

THE ADVENTURE CONTINUES

Find some private, comfortable space in your home or wherever you happen to be. You'll need a pen, a Bible, and this book. (Well, obviously you wouldn't be reading this if you didn't have the book.) You might also want a dictionary, a Bible dictionary, or Web access so you can look stuff up.

Find Psalm 23 in your Bible. You'll be studying the entire psalm. But don't worry—it's not long. Using the S.T.O.P. method, study Psalm 23 and journal your insights at each step:

1. What does it SAY?
   (Think about what the words actually say, and look up the meanings of any words you don't know.)

2. What were the TIMES?
   (Consider what the times were like when the passage was written. What was the time period in history? What events were happening? What was important to people at that time? Look stuff up if you need to.)

3. What did it mean ORIGINALLY?
   (Think about who wrote it, who it was written for, and what
   it would have meant to the first people who read it.)

4. What does it mean for me PERSONALLY?
   (Think about how the Bible passage applies to you. Knowing
   what you learned in the other steps, what can you learn and
   act on in your own life?)

So how did it work? What insights did you gain during your
Bible study? Do you see or understand this passage differently?
Hopefully this study showed you how this kind of Bible study can
change the way you read and understand the Bible. And understanding the Bible can change the way you live.

As you continue to do this kind of Bible study, here are some
other Bible passages to explore: Genesis 22:1-19; Psalm 139; Isaiah
9:1-7; Ezekiel 37:1-14; Matthew 6:5-15; John 1:1-18; Romans 12:1-8;
1 Corinthians 13; Galatians 5:1-15; Ephesians 6:10-20; and Philippians
2:1-11. As you study, you can use the journal pages at the back of
this book (pages 53-63) to write about what you learn.

CHAPTER 3

EQUIPPED FOR ADVENTURE

Have you ever been in your pastor's office? Does your pastor have rows and rows of huge books with titles that sound so boring to you that you're sure you'd fall into a coma if you opened one of them? Have you visited a Bible study website and seen lists of resources like commentaries, synoptic gospels, and — perhaps the most intimidating — *exhaustive* concordances? Well, these resources are Bible study tools. And these tools just might not be as boring as you think they are.

Most people have no clue about the tools that are available to help them understand and apply the Bible. They may open their Bibles, read the first thing they see, and close them again without understanding anything. Or they may rely on devotionals to interpret Scripture for them, without knowing they can learn to interpret Scripture themselves. But they don't have to do it on their own!

And you don't have to study the Bible on your own either. This chapter will arm you with a working knowledge of Bible study tools. With this knowledge, you can take advantage of these tools in your own study, learning to understand Scripture on your own.

STARTING THE JOURNEY

I know this sounds weird, but there really is a good reason for it: Grab a bag or a pillowcase or something you can use to carry stuff. Then take a minute to walk around your home or your room or the circus tent or wherever you happen to be. As you walk around, find about ten things to put in your bag. You can fill your bag with just about anything: clothes, toilet paper, tape, string, sunglasses, a fork, towels, batteries, soap, pencils . . . whatever.

Now it's time to use your imagination. Sit down with your bag and dump it out on the floor. You're now stranded on a deserted island, and all you have with you are the supplies you collected in your bag. You must think of a way to use those supplies to either get off the island or contact someone to help you. I'll give you a few minutes to come up with ideas.

Okay, now put everything back.

TRY THIS!

This is even more fun with a friend!

Find someone to do this with you. Each of you should fill a bag with ten things. Then have a contest to see who can come up with the most ideas for getting off the island (or finding help). Then switch bags and see if you can come up with more ideas.

I hope you'll never be stranded on a deserted island. And if you ever are, I hope you'll have better supplies — like a boat, a map, and some clean underwear.

The point here is simple: Survival is all about having the right supplies. And so is successful Bible study.

"Supplies?" you may ask. "What kind of supplies do I need for Bible study?"

Well, I'm glad you asked. With Bible study, it's important to have tools. And not just tools — the right tools. The right Bible study tools will help you in every step of the S.T.O.P. process. Read on to find out more about some specific Bible study tools and how they can benefit you.

IN-DEPTH EXPLORATION

Here's a list of some of the basic Bible study tools everyone should learn how to use:

- Bible commentaries—Written by Bible scholars and experts, they teach us what other people have learned and discovered as they have studied the Bible.
- Christian websites (such as www.biblemaster.com, www .biblestudy.com, and www.biblestudytools.net)—These are great places to find all kinds of helpful information about the Bible.
- Bible dictionaries—They're like other dictionaries, but they're focused on words found in Scripture. They tell us what biblical words mean.
- Bible encyclopedias—They tell us more about the people, places, customs, and events described in the Bible.
- Study Bibles—They include Bible scholars' and experts' notes about specific verses, words, and passages. These notes are found throughout the Bible so you can read them as you read Scripture.
- Concordances—They help us find where specific words are used in the Bible. You can look up a word and find all the places in the Bible where that word appears.

Before you keep reading, get your hands on at least one of these Bible study tools. You'll need it to practice and learn. You might want to start by going to one of the suggested websites. If you want to try something else instead (or you want to learn about more than one tool), ask your pastor if you can borrow one. Or ask your parents if they have a study Bible at home.

Once you've found at least one study tool, spend several minutes getting to know it. Figure out how it works and what it does. Think about why people have created this Bible study tool. Consider how this tool can help you as you study the Bible.

Okay, enough of that. It's great to know how these Bible study tools work, but it's even better to actually use them. It's time to practice using at least one of these tools in some actual Bible study.

BIBLE DISCOVERY

Find Exodus 32:1-14 in your Bible. Now, depending on what Bible study tool you have available, see if there's a part that specifically relates to Exodus 32:1-14. Use the S.T.O.P. method and your Bible study tool(s) to study the passage. As you study, answer these questions:

1. What does it SAY?

2. What were the TIMES?

3. What did it mean ORIGINALLY?

4. What does it mean for me PERSONALLY?

TRY THIS!

If you have a friend nearby, you can learn twice as much. Try study-ing this passage separately. Then, after you've gone through all four steps, tell each other what you learned. This will work especially well if you use different Bible study tools.

Now go tell someone else what you learned. Seriously. Talk to your mom, call a friend, visit your grandma, or e-mail your pastor. He or she will love it!

THE ADVENTURE CONTINUES

So you've figured out how to use Bible study tools. You can go deeper in your Bible study. You can learn more than you could on your own. You can benefit from the wisdom and knowledge of people who have devoted their lives to understanding God's Word. This is worth more practice. Here's what to do next. Spend a few moments writing down one question you have about the Bible — something that has been confusing you or a particular pas-sage that you don't understand.

Because you'll be looking in the Bible for an answer to this question, it should be specifically related to Scripture. It should be the kind of question you can answer by looking in the Bible.

For example, a good question might be "Why did Jesus have to die?" or "What does the Bible say about violence?" or "What do the Beatitudes really mean?" Write your question here:

Okay, now decide which Bible study tool you can use to help you answer the question you wrote down. Then go to work. Use your tool to find in the Bible the answer to your question. Write about what you learn:

This is probably a good time to pray. Thank God for showing you his truth in the Bible. Ask him to continue to reveal and clarify his truth to you as you study.

CHAPTER 4

HITTING THE TRAIL

You've learned so much already. You have a new method and new tools at your disposal. You're beginning to understand what you read in the Bible. But what's the point if it doesn't make any difference in your life?

That's an important question. The ultimate purpose of Bible study is not to simply read the Bible or even to understand it; it's to experience change in your life, bringing you closer to God and God's plans for you. If you don't understand the fourth step of Bible study, for you Bible study will be robotic, impersonal, and weak. Bible study is incomplete without personal application. This chapter will equip you to take this important step in Bible study and let God's Word change the way you live on an ongoing basis.

STARTING THE JOURNEY

Think about food labels for a moment. That's right, food labels. When was the last time you read a list of ingredients? Weird stuff, huh? Do you even know what polysorbate is? How about hypromellose? In fact, does anyone know?

At some point, you've probably read the ingredient label of something you were eating and wondered exactly what those ingredients were. But have you ever read a list of ingredients and tried to guess what the food was? Just for fun, see if you can figure out what food has these ingredients:

Sugar, enriched flour (wheat flour, niacin, reduced iron, thiamine mono-nitrate [Vitamin B₁], riboflavin [Vitamin B₂], folic acid), high oleic canola oil and/or palm oil and/or canola oil, cocoa (processed with alkali), high fructose corn syrup, baking soda, cornstarch, salt, soy lecithin (emulsifier), vanillin, chocolate.

Any guesses? The answer is Oreo cookies.
Here's another one:

Corn syrup, sugar, modified cornstarch, water, gelatin, tetrasodium pyrophosphate (whipping aid), artificial flavor, artificial color.

Give up? Marshmallows.
One more:

Sugar, corn syrup, partially hydrogenated soybean oil, citric acid, titanium dioxide, condensed skim milk, cocoa, whey, artificial and natural flavors, Soya lecithin, artificial colors, turmeric coloring.

The answer: Tootsie Pops!

It's not easy to guess the ingredients in these foods, is it? That's probably because you don't pay much attention to what's in these kinds of foods. If you're eating a Tootsie Pop, you think of it as a Tootsie Pop, not a combination of titanium dioxide and condensed skim milk. As long as you know it's edible, it's not dangerous, and it tastes good, the individual ingredients probably aren't that important to you.

But if you think about it, the ingredients really are important. Without tetrasodium pyrophosphate, you just don't have a marshmallow. So even if you don't think a lot about individual ingredients, your life wouldn't be the same without them.

Believe it or not, ingredient labels really do relate to Bible study. The final step of Bible study is sort of like understanding an ingredient label. Let's discover how.

IN-DEPTH EXPLORATION

Just as you can break foods into lists of their individual ingredients, you can break Bible passages into principles and specific ideas of what they mean for you.

Take James 3:9-10, for example:

With the tongue we praise our Lord and Father, and with it we curse men, who have been made in God's likeness. Out of the same mouth come praise and cursing. My brothers, this should not be.

After reading a passage from the Bible, we can draw a principle from it, sort of summarizing something that passage says. Here's a principle you could draw out of what you just read:

The way we talk to others should glorify God, building others up.

That's the first part of application. Now for the second part. Once you've drawn out a principle, you can then draw some personal applications from that principle. In other words, you can come up with some specific ways that principle applies to you. For example, from this principle we can draw these applications:

- I should encourage my family.
- I should stop talking about people behind their backs.

There's one more part to this application process: Act on what you learn! That's the most important thing you can do. That's what makes our lives change. For now, though, practice drawing principles and applications from verses. If you get really good at that, you'll have a lot to act on.

Try this application matching game. Read the following Bible passages. Then look at the list of principles. Choose the one that you think fits each passage and write its number underneath the Bible reference. Choose the two applications that best fit that principle and write their letters underneath as well. When you're finished, you can check your answers on page 46.

PASSAGES

Proverbs 3:5-6
    1 Principle: _____
    2 Applications: _____
Matthew 5:14-16
    1 Principle: _____
    2 Applications: _____
Romans 12:2
    1 Principle: _____
    2 Applications: _____
Philippians 2:3-4
    1 Principle: _____
    2 Applications: _____

PRINCIPLES

1. Your life should be a clear light to others, leading them to God.
2. Live unselfishly, caring about others.
3. Be nice to other people so they'll give you gifts.
4. Follow God's way instead of the ways of the world around you.
5. Your body is not your own — it is God's, so treat it right.
6. Trust God instead of depending on yourself.

APPLICATIONS

a. I should leave the last piece of pizza for someone else to enjoy.
b. I should choose to obey God, even when it doesn't make sense to me.
c. I should let others know I'm a Christian.
d. I should get eight hours of sleep every night.
e. I shouldn't brag or act as though I'm the best.
f. I should stand up for what's right, even if it means going against the crowd.
g. I shouldn't miss the season finale of my favorite TV show.
h. I should ask God to help me decide what to do after graduation.

i. I should always wear sunscreen.

j. I should act in a way that makes people want to know God.

k. I should try to be like Jesus instead of being popular.

How did you do? Hopefully you're getting pretty good at this. This fourth step of the S.T.O.P. method (discovering what Scripture means to you personally) is extremely important in Bible study. In fact, without it, the other three steps don't mean much. So if you're struggling with this one, consider going back to the application matching game. Review the answers until they make sense to you. It might help to ask someone else to help you understand how the principles and applications were drawn out of those verses.

Once the application matching game makes sense to you, move on to the next section to go to the next level.

BIBLE DISCOVERY

It's time for some more serious practice. Now is your chance to put the whole thing together. Use the S.T.O.P. method to study Matthew 22:1-14. As you go through each step, write your insights in the space provided. When you get to the fourth step, you'll practice finding some principles and applications in the Bible passage.

1. What does it SAY?

2. What were the TIMES?

3. What did it mean ORIGINALLY?

4. What does it mean for me PERSONALLY?

TRY THIS!

Try this with a friend. Use the S.T.O.P. method to study Matthew 22:1-14 together. When you get to the fourth step, stop working together.

Each of you tackle the fourth step alone. Individually come up with a principle and at least one application drawn from Matthew 22:1-14. Then play a game to guess what principles and applications you came up with.

You've played the game Hangman, right? Play it with your friend to guess your principles and applications. On a piece of paper or a dry-erase board, draw a dash to represent each letter of your principle. Leave a space between words. Let your friend guess a letter

---

at a time until he or she figures out the principle, and then switch places. Try the same thing with your applications.

Another idea is to play a game of Charades instead of Hangman. Act out a principle or application while your friend guesses what you came up with.

Hopefully you see how important the application step is in Bible study. It is something you can and should do as you study the Bible on your own. Of course, you must make sure your principles and applications accurately reflect what God wants to say to you. Some of the best ways to make sure are to pray as you study the Bible and to test your principles and applications by comparing them to what the Bible says in other passages. God does not contradict himself, and neither does his Word.

It should be easy to see how this kind of Bible application can affect your life. If you act on what you learn, God's Spirit will make you into a new person! This is worth a little more practice.

THE ADVENTURE CONTINUES

Find a comfortable, quiet place to hang out for a while. Make sure you have a pen or pencil. You might want to play some reflective or worshipful music.

Comfy? Then spend a few moments in prayer, asking God to guide you as you study and seek to apply his Word.

Okay, now choose a favorite Bible passage or verse. If you're not sure what to pick, here are some ideas:

- Genesis 1:1
- John 3:16
- Romans 8:28
- Galatians 5:22-23
- 1 John 4:7-8
- Revelation 3:20

Read and study your passage or verse. Then in the following space, write at least one principle that comes from what you read:

Now write down some specific applications for you personally, as many as come to mind:

You may have written several application ideas. If so, that's great. You have a lot of potential ways your life can change. But in Bible study, it's always a good idea to choose just one or two application ideas to focus on. Trying to apply a Scripture passage in every possible way will only lead to frustration and confusion. So go ahead and focus on one for now. You can always come back and focus on the others at another time. Write down one way you're going to *act on* one of the application ideas you wrote about:

Now take action! This is where the rubber meets the road. The ultimate purpose of Bible study is not just to read the Bible or even to understand it; the ultimate purpose is to experience change in your life. As you draw out principles and applications and then act on them, your life will change and bring more glory to God.

CHAPTER 5

EXTREME ADVENTURE

After working through the first four chapters of this book, you should have a good basic understanding of the importance of Bible study and how you can study God's Word on your own. But this understanding is important only if you actually use what you've learned.

This chapter is full of ideas to help you study the Bible on your own. To flex your muscles, pick one or more of the special Bible study projects that follow. Then use the journal pages (pages 53-76) to record your insights as you study the Bible passages with the S.T.O.P. method. Once you've used all the ideas in this book, you'll find yourself ready to dive deeper into any Bible passage. You'll be well on your way to making Bible study a lifelong habit.

You'll be glad you started this lifelong journey. As you study God's Word, you'll find wisdom, truth, and knowledge of God that will change your life. Your journey has only begun!

IDEAS FOR BIBLE STUDY PROJECTS

1. Choose a favorite passage to dig into and really understand, using the S.T.O.P. method. Here are some ideas for Bible passages you might choose from (you'll find pages devoted just to these passages on pages 53-63), or choose your own passage (see pages 64-76).

- Genesis 22:1-19
- Psalm 139
- Isaiah 9:1-7
- Ezekiel 37:1-14
- Matthew 6:5-15
- John 1:1-18
- Romans 12:1-8
- 1 Corinthians 13
- Galatians 5:1-15
- Ephesians 6:10-20
- Philippians 2:1-11

2. Choose a word or concept and study several Bible passages to get a good understanding of what it means. Here are some words and concepts you might choose from:

- Atonement
- Community
- Forgiveness
- Grace
- Heaven
- Holiness
- Justice
- Justification
- Law
- Love
- Mercy

- Prophecy
- Righteousness
- Sacrifice
- Service
- Spiritual gifts

3. Choose a person described in the Bible and study key Bible passages to get to know that person and God's work in his or her life. Here are some people you might choose from:

- Aaron
- Abigail
- Amos
- Barnabas
- Deborah
- Esther
- Gideon
- Jacob
- Jeremiah
- John the Baptist
- Mary, the mother of Jesus
- Miriam
- Moses
- Nehemiah
- Paul
- Peter
- Ruth

4. Choose a cultural or historical force or event and study key Bible passages to understand how that factor was present in Bible times. Here are some forces or events you might choose from:

- War
- Slavery

- Roman Empire
- Persecution
- Hellenization
- The Exodus
- Drought
- Dreams
- Sickness
- Money
- Birth

S.T.O.P. METHOD FOR BIBLE STUDY

When you're doing Bible study, refer to this page as a reminder of the S.T.O.P. method and how it works.

> What does it SAY?
> *Think about what the words actually say, and look up the meanings of any words you don't know.*

> What were the TIMES?
> *Consider what the times were like when the passage was written. What was the time period in history? What events were happening? What was important to people at that time? It's a great idea to look up this information in a reliable source.*

> What did it mean ORIGINALLY?
> *Consider what the Bible passage meant when it was written. Think about who wrote it, who it was written for, and what it would have meant to people then.*

> What does it mean for me PERSONALLY?
> *Think about how the Bible passage applies to you. Knowing what you learned in the other steps, what can you learn and act on in your own life?*

BIBLE STUDY OUTLINE — GENESIS 22:1-19

Use the S.T.O.P. method to study Genesis 22:1-19, and record your insights below.

Date:

> What does it SAY?

> What were the TIMES?

> What did it mean ORIGINALLY?

> What does it mean for me PERSONALLY?

BIBLE STUDY OUTLINE — PSALM 139

Use the S.T.O.P. method to study Psalm 139, and record your insights below.

Date:

> What does it SAY?

> What were the TIMES?

> What did it mean ORIGINALLY?

> What does it mean for me PERSONALLY?

BIBLE STUDY OUTLINE — ISAIAH 9:1-7

Use the S.T.O.P. method to study Isaiah 9:1-7, and record your insights below.

Date:

> What does it SAY?

> What were the TIMES?

> What did it mean ORIGINALLY?

> What does it mean for me PERSONALLY?

BIBLE STUDY OUTLINE — EZEKIEL 37:1-14

Use the S.T.O.P. method to study Ezekiel 37:1-14, and record your insights below.

Date:

> What does it SAY?

> What were the TIMES?

> What did it mean ORIGINALLY?

> What does it mean for me PERSONALLY?

BIBLE STUDY OUTLINE — MATTHEW 6:5-15

Use the S.T.O.P. method to study Matthew 6:5-15, and record your insights below.

Date:

> What does it SAY?

> What were the TIMES?

> What did it mean ORIGINALLY?

> What does it mean for me PERSONALLY?

BIBLE STUDY OUTLINE — JOHN 1:1-18

Use the S.T.O.P. method to study John 1:1-18, and record your insights below.

Date:

> What does it SAY?

> What were the TIMES?

> What did it mean ORIGINALLY?

> What does it mean for me PERSONALLY?

BIBLE STUDY OUTLINE — ROMANS 12:1-8

Use the S.T.O.P. method to study Romans 12:1-8, and record your insights below.

Date:

> What does it SAY?

> What were the TIMES?

> What did it mean ORIGINALLY?

> What does it mean for me PERSONALLY?

BIBLE STUDY OUTLINE — 1 CORINTHIANS 13

Use the S.T.O.P. method to study 1 Corinthians 13, and record your insights below.

Date:

> What does it SAY?

> What were the TIMES?

> What did it mean ORIGINALLY?

> What does it mean for me PERSONALLY?

BIBLE STUDY OUTLINE — GALATIANS 5:1-15

Use the S.T.O.P. method to study Galatians 5:1-15, and record your insights below.

Date:

> What does it SAY?

> What were the TIMES?

> What did it mean ORIGINALLY?

> What does it mean for me PERSONALLY?

BIBLE STUDY OUTLINE — EPHESIANS 6:10-20

Use the S.T.O.P. method to study Ephesians 6:10-20, and record your insights below.

Date:

> What does it SAY?

> What were the TIMES?

> What did it mean ORIGINALLY?

> What does it mean for me PERSONALLY?

BIBLE STUDY OUTLINE — PHILIPPIANS 2:1-11

Use the S.T.O.P. method to study Philippians 2:1-11, and record your insights below.

Date:

> What does it SAY?

> What were the TIMES?

> What did it mean ORIGINALLY?

> What does it mean for me PERSONALLY?

BIBLE STUDY OUTLINE _____

Use the S.T.O.P. method to study a passage of your choice, and record your insights below.

Date:

> What does it SAY?

> What were the TIMES?

> What did it mean ORIGINALLY?

> What does it mean for me PERSONALLY?

BIBLE STUDY OUTLINE _____

Use the S.T.O.P. method to study a passage of your choice, and record your insights below.

Date:

> What does it SAY?

> What were the TIMES?

> What did it mean ORIGINALLY?

> What does it mean for me PERSONALLY?

BIBLE STUDY OUTLINE _____

Use the S.T.O.P. method to study a passage of your choice, and record your insights below.

Date:

> > What does it SAY?

> > What were the TIMES?

> > What did it mean ORIGINALLY?

> > What does it mean for me PERSONALLY?

BIBLE STUDY OUTLINE _____

Use the S.T.O.P. method to study a passage of your choice, and record your insights below.

Date:

> What does it SAY?

> What were the TIMES?

> What did it mean ORIGINALLY?

> What does it mean for me PERSONALLY?

BIBLE STUDY OUTLINE _____

Use the S.T.O.P. method to study a passage of your choice, and record your insights below.

Date:

> What does it SAY?

> What were the TIMES?

> What did it mean ORIGINALLY?

> What does it mean for me PERSONALLY?

BIBLE STUDY OUTLINE _____

Use the S.T.O.P. method to study a passage of your choice, and record your insights below.

Date:

> What does it SAY?

> What were the TIMES?

> What did it mean ORIGINALLY?

> What does it mean for me PERSONALLY?

BIBLE STUDY OUTLINE _____

Use the S.T.O.P. method to study a passage of your choice, and record your insights below.

Date:

> What does it SAY?

> What were the TIMES?

> What did it mean ORIGINALLY?

> What does it mean for me PERSONALLY?

BIBLE STUDY OUTLINE _____

Use the S.T.O.P. method to study a passage of your choice, and record your insights below.

Date:

> What does it SAY?

> What were the TIMES?

> What did it mean ORIGINALLY?

> What does it mean for me PERSONALLY?

BIBLE STUDY OUTLINE _____

Use the S.T.O.P. method to study a passage of your choice, and record your insights below.

Date:

> What does it SAY?

> What were the TIMES?

> What did it mean ORIGINALLY?

> What does it mean for me PERSONALLY?

BIBLE STUDY OUTLINE _____

Use the S.T.O.P. method to study a passage of your choice, and record your insights below.

Date:

> What does it SAY?

> What were the TIMES?

> What did it mean ORIGINALLY?

> What does it mean for me PERSONALLY?

BIBLE STUDY OUTLINE _____

Use the S.T.O.P. method to study a passage of your choice, and record your insights below.

Date:

> What does it SAY?

> What were the TIMES?

> What did it mean ORIGINALLY?

> What does it mean for me PERSONALLY?

BIBLE STUDY OUTLINE _____

Use the S.T.O.P. method to study a passage of your choice, and record your insights below.

Date:

> What does it SAY?

> What were the TIMES?

> What did it mean ORIGINALLY?

> What does it mean for me PERSONALLY?

BIBLE STUDY OUTLINE _____

Use the S.T.O.P. method to study a passage of your choice, and record your insights below.

Date:

> What does it SAY?

> What were the TIMES?

> What did it mean ORIGINALLY?

> What does it mean for me PERSONALLY?

DISCUSSION GUIDE

If you're using this book with a group, try meeting five times and covering one chapter in each meeting. Use these discussion questions to get your group talking.

CHAPTER 1

> What was the most surprising thing you learned about the Bible by reading this chapter?

> What makes the Bible worthy of our trust?

> Why is it important to know how to follow the "map" in the Bible?

> How has the Bible been useful in your life or the life of someone you know?

CHAPTER 2

> How is reading the Bible sometimes similar to reading a coded message?

> How could the S.T.O.P. method affect the way you study and understand the Bible?

> What did you learn as you studied Psalm 23?

> How might this kind of Bible study affect your life?

CHAPTER 3

> Why do you think people have created Bible study tools?
> How can Bible study tools help you?
> What makes a Bible study tool trustworthy?
> Which of these tools do you think might be most helpful in your personal Bible study?

CHAPTER 4

> Why is the fourth step of the S.T.O.P. method so important?
> What principles and applications did you come up with when you studied Matthew 22:1-14? How about when you chose your own passage to study?
> How can we make sure our principles and applications accurately reflect what God wants to say to us?
> How might this kind of Bible application affect your life?
> How will your life change as you apply what you learned today?

CHAPTER 5

> Which Bible study project will you choose to complete? Why?
> What have you learned in your personal Bible study this week?
> How is the power of God's Word affecting your life?

> > >

AUTHOR

AMY SIMPSON is an executive director for *Christianity Today International*. Her background includes a thirteen-year career in Christian publishing and a lifetime of church ministry, including a decade in youth ministry. She is the author of numerous resources for Christian ministry, including *Diving Deep: Experiencing Jesus Through Spiritual Disciplines.* Amy lives in Illinois with her husband, Trevor, and their two fantastic kids.

More Great TH1NK Titles!

Ask Me Anything 2
J. Budziszewski

978-1-60006-193-6
1-60006-193-1

In his sequel, the professor returns with an all-new collection of insights on the hot topics facing today's teens and twenty-somethings. This time he takes on even hotter, tougher, and more piercing questions than before.

Renovation of the Heart
Dallas Willard and Randy Frazee

978-1-57683-730-6
1-57683-730-0

With easy-to-understand examples, review questions, and explanations of keywords, this book will help you understand one of the most complicated and important lessons of life: putting on the character of Christ.

Own Your Faith
Mark Tabb

978-1-60006-097-7
1-60006-097-8

How can you learn to think for yourself and make your faith your own—not the faith of your parents, youth leaders, or pastor? This insightful yet humorous guide will lead you through the process of grappling with and living out your convictions in a postmodern world.

To order copies, visit your local Christian bookstore,
call NavPress at 1-800-366-7788, or log on to www.navpress.com.

To locate a Christian bookstore near you, call 1-800-991-7747.